TWO SIDES OF THE SAME COIN

By: Sheldon Gilton

DEDICATION

This book is for men and women who know that relationships aren't just black and white. When it comes to love and relationships; we are all grey. We are all one in the same. We just have different stories to tell.
-Sheldon "Low-Key" Gilton

CONTENTS

ACKNOWLEDGMENTS

Above all, I would like to thank God for blessing me with this talent and love for writing. He put the thought in my mind to touch people through my words so all glory, honor, and praise goes to the Most High. Special thanks to Ernest Gray aka "Ernest GQ" for designing the front and back cover for this book. I wish him the best in all of his endeavors. I also just want to thank all of my family and friends. They are my drive and motivation I need to keep pursuing my passion. Thank you to everyone who participated in the interviews conducted to implement this concept. I really appreciate each of you. Special thanks go out to Lemarcus Jackson for providing me a sample of his work to be featured in this book. I also want to thank everyone else who supported the idea and my writing ever since my first publication. It means so much to me and I hope to have equal if not more support for future projects.

The Nice Guy

My favorite show as a kid was Tom & Jerry
because it really showed me; if you want
something you go and get it.
I apply that concept to everyday life
experiences, especially when it comes to my
relationships with women.
I am Malik.
My interactions with women are a game of
cat and mouse. Soon as I think I'm close to
having them in my clutches, they hit the
clutch and immediately shift gears.
I'm left in their rearview.
I'm left with dreams of her that won't ever
be right as I'm looking at her rear view.
It's a nice sight for sore eyes that won't be
clear because I got caught in her jet stream.
She drifts pass me in her red bottom pumps
breaking necks severing my head from my
spine.
This girl is literally making me lose my mind.
I'm losing my head over heels she wears to
make her claves pop.
Bursting my bubble; to think she'll ever go
for a guy like me.
From what I can see, the bad boy is what
she finds most appealing.
If one would give me the chance, I would
give her a ring to make her cheeks rosy.
She dances across the posies I gave her
turning my dreams into ashes;
Ashes I fall down as she walks away with
someone who won't do right by her.
He treats her like a female dog and a garden

tool.

She is his hose pipe.

He gives all of his hoes pipe as they provide
a fertile garden for his seeds to sprout.

I just don't understand and it's very
frustrating.

Most of these women know the guy isn't the
one, yet they insist on being number two.

Possibly three; I'm sure she knows he has
more than just her on his team.

He's the quarterback and she's just one of
the wide receivers, widely receiving accurate
passes until her legs are field goal post.

He's in the end zone.

I'm not the type to just want to get in her
end zone and score.

My intentions are worth more than that.

I'm a well-dressed gentleman, who knows I
can't always be a gentle man.

I am firm.

I'm trying to employ a secretary.

If she has any secrets, I want her to tell me.

I am an impenetrable vault with her heart
within my walls.

I'm the type to open doors for her to walk
through.

I take my time as I take time to provide to
girl with a feeling of something new.

The feeling is foreign and she may not know
the role of being a lover, but I'm
Christopher Columbus.

I will help her discover that she can be Miss
America.

No other girl can compare in contrast to
her.

I'll put her on a pedestal and remain at the
bottom to catch her if she falls.
I give her all of me and make her believe in a
love that was once legend.
Her faults don't make her deadline, because
in my mind, her imperfections make her
perfect.
I sit here every day analyzing her
complications and compile ideas to put in
application towards us growing more as one.
I want to lay and pray as we prey on each
other's lust for love and quench our thirst
with the other's affection.
If she's underwater and drowning in life's
sea, I'll bring her to the surface and make
her see that I'm not going to let her go so
easily.
I'm here for when her love calls and I'll
answer, but I wonder will anyone answer
me?
For the longest dial tones serenade me in the
depths of the night when I'm only being
patient to find Mrs. Right.
I don't think as a man we are truly living
until we find one woman that makes a
whole, or at least I thought that until I met
this girl name Nicole.

Nicole

I often wondered about the Seven Wonders
of the World, but in my mind there are really
eight.
Nicole, I wish the golden arches of the
Golden Gate could bridge me to the
heavens where you reside.
Once there, seven angels would sound their
seven trumpets releasing the seven seals that
seal you to heaven so you may be free to
bless the Earth.
She is the stars that I connect with my finger
to form new constellations that consume
majority of the Milky Way.
She is a supernova that explodes her beauty
to the atmosphere in cosmic rays that appear
as auroras in the northern hemisphere.
Everyone can hear the angels in heaven
clamoring over her magnificence.
She is the angel of beauty that shrouds the
world causing plants to beautify and
cultivate the land.
The brightness from fireworks are minute
compared to the hours of work God put
into making her.
Her northern lights shine over the Great
Pyramid of Giza causing me to become
inebriated and fall out of the sky.
I grab a ray from the sun and gently stroke
the clouds with the two of us under an old
oak.
Nicole's voice caused an orchestra in heaven
glorifying God. It creates earthquakes every

time she spoke.
She stands tall with open arms like the
Christ the Redeemer statue in Rio that I just
want to embrace.
My fingertips crave to touch her face.
The anticipation makes my heart race more
than a couple beats a minute.
Nicole, I wish I could admit it to you face to
face that you are my Taj Mahal.
A castle for comfort and sanctuary with
columns for our love to congregate; hoping
that our seeds will sprout to and populate
every room this palace possesses.
No great wall will block me from
penetrating the heart of the fine china that
lies behind it.
Nicole, you make me go out my mind as
though I could be brain dead.
I return to a cerebrum full of life inhabited
by you instead.
You create a barrier that no foreign or
domestic terrorist can penetrate to terrorize.
You enrich my mind with truth and honesty.
The effect is it makes my blood rush to my
heart filling each cavity within so there is no
longer a hole.
With you Nicole, I feel whole.
She is the Great Barrier Reef because she is
beautiful and radiant.
She is calm and she is forever.
Within her skin are different walks of life.
Her roots run miles through the earth's
surface making her deeper than any ocean's
depth.
Her love fills the Grand Canyon causing it

to overflow like Niagara Falls.
I can't help but fall for this unique girl.
I shine on campus in front of other females,
but I can help but revolve around her world.
Everything about her is natural and it makes
me think of South Africa.
Her heart beat is in sync with the mating
calls of the animals.
Bongo drums introduce her performance as
South Africa is her stage; she pliés spreading
love across the land.
The gazelles are her band providing the
music that she dances too.
She is a ballerina as her pirouettes cause the
sun to set to give rise to the spotlight moon
for opening night.
She graces the stage performing a romantic
love ballet underneath the setting rays.
She is natural.
She is a part of nature.
She displays her true essence in the attitude
pose that I want to capture and post on my
wall, but I wonder if she even notices me at
all.

The Approach

I don't think she notice me, yet I pay
attention to her.
I spend time attentively articulating ways to
make that change.
She jams Beyoncé's "Drunk in Love".
How I would love to be intoxicated
everyday if she was the drink in my cup.
I need to stop analyzing this girl from a
distance and make a move, but what am I
going to say?
I need to think about this approach.
In order to make this prize my possession
and display my trophy, I need to bypass her
friends.
My chances fall slim.
The outcome of success is shady.
A female's friends know when a guy is
coming to spit game; they are immediately
ready to throw salt and watch you marinate
in shame.
I have to dodge the bitter friend.
She gets sour just from the idea of a man.
She's the chick that comes with a fee you
see, comparing all men to feces.
She not as bad as the friend that will bust
jokes to crack a man's confidence.
She's usually high maintenance, but lacking
common sense to pay attention to her body
trending in the streets.
Simply put, she can't maintain the idea that
no one will want to purchase a building
that's already been demolished.

Then the, "We Got to Go Friend" is always
there to pull her away.
So she already has obstacles ready to cock
block, but this cock can't be blocked by tight
walls securing that pearl. I'm determined to
break them down to get to my treasure.
One day, I spotted her.
She was alone coming from class; my eyes
fixated on her like a hawk as she walked
pass.
I immediately tried to compute what I
wanted to say while also trying to keep my
"Johnson" micro soft because the way she
was looking gave me a hard drive.
I just hoped I could steer this conversation
in the right direction so I don't end up
looking lost.
I caught her and inquired about her writing
poetry; she said she does write.
I suggested a place she might like that
conducts open mic.
She said she would check it out.
How I would like to purchase a pound of
her fruit if only I could be the apple of her
eye.
She asked for my name.
What I wanted to say was,
"I am Boston.
A marathon of thoughts about you go
through my head on a daily.
I am the air you inhale to make you exhale
the tar and nicotine received from nickels
that act like teens.
I am the only one in your late text, talking
about activities involving a latex; I am the

thoughts you key in your keyboard when
everyone in your contacts keep you bored.
The emoticons you send are bail bonds
releasing your life sentenced feelings.
When we are together, sparks fly turning us
into flies in an electric lamp; quite shocking
to others that we last even when our ground
is damp."
Instead, I just said Malik.
Nicole gave me a smile and let me know
next time, make sure to speak.
Followed by, we can hang out sometime.
Thank you God for Nicole. She is a vista I
would print and post on my wall just to gaze
at her magnificence.
Well, after I file her empty cabinets.
I dream of cabin nights spent looking at the
stars, but that can happen in due time.
I hope we turn into something more.
Hopefully, we can intersect and my feelings
are expressed to her in the right angle.
That way she is acute so we don't have to be
obtuse and she can bear my grizzly
emotions.

Quality Time

It was a Monday.
I caught her attention after class.
I reeled her in as I began to ask her out on a
date.
One would swear I was having sex, because
I was a virgin at asking a girl out.
I didn't know the in's and out's to it.
I didn't know if I should be smooth and
spring it on her gently, or be brash and show
her I'm eager to spend some cash.
No, I don't want her to think I'm trying to
buy her so she can pay me some attention.
I decided to ask her for a walk in the park
accompanied by snowballs.
Yeah, that seemed to be the simplest route.
Hopefully, at the end of the road, we will
have molded.
We will be shaped and fired, so our unity
will last forever. Eventually, I work up the
nerve to ask her.
When I did she was quiet.
The doubt made me assume she would say
"no", but she said "Yes".
She definitely made an ass out of me.
I guess that's what I get for assuming.
We agreed it would be this coming Friday.
That whole week, I wish it would come soon
so I could be satisfied spending time with
her. Friday came.
We met at the park.
She wore a floral dress; she must be in tuned
with nature. The sun's rays shined through

her natural hair to her bronze skin.
It was reflected like her pores were iron ores
containing diamonds that refracted the light
through lens. I could vividly see her glowing.
I only stood there in awe.
It was like the world was place on pause for
me to witness that moment.
All Nicole could do was smile.
We sat on the benches and talked about life
and our places in it.
I was being myself.
I didn't want to be the guy who flips like a
cd changer.
She see these syllables I spit.
I figure she's one who loves an articulate
man.
The glass of our conversation was filled with
humor.
I actually made her laugh as I poured into
her who I was. She reciprocated, but I
flipped the script when I informed her of
my intentions.
My eye are tint.
I shun out all other women and it's only her
I see.
For the longest I admired her from across
the yard.
I was too afraid to make a move, until now.
She just listened attentively.
She placed her hand on top of mine.
Our eyes locked like padlocks.
Neither of us wanted to look away as the
silence was comforting.
I didn't want this quality to end.
She liked how I checked her in this comfort

inn.

From then on, she looked forward to the
weekend.

Every week ends with us doing something
together.

I looked back occasionally and wonder why
it took me so long to get her.

We go to the mall and I help her pick out
outfits. Sometimes I thought she out fit the
clothes she tried on. We'd go bowling or
random walks.

Majority of the time we enjoyed solitude.

I felt solely in tuned with her and her
heartbeat; the both of ours appeared to be in
sync.

Hopefully neither of us will be crying rivers,
because the other wanted something that
way.

Nicole touches me in a way that I believe
she's already mine, but in my mind I feels
she's not, because I haven't even kissed her
yet.

The Meeting

For a while, Nicole and I been conversing.
I imagine kissing her after our dates,
becoming chucked across the sky like a
shooting star.
She's the one I wished on as we gaze into
each other's eyes, because we're tailored for
one another.
I hope she's not getting bored with me,
because I haven't made a move to finally
have us in check.
In my mind, I keep pawning my way into
how I will approach kissing her.
If I could only muster up the nerve, I
wouldn't have to worry about us ending.
It's Valentine's Day.
I have something special planned.
I'm going to do it tonight.
I pick her up around six.
She walked out her home looking like a
vixen.
The black dress displayed her treacherous
curves that raveled near her waistline.
Her hips are hollow points fired at everyone
that witnessed her killing that dress.
Her lips resembled rubies.
She already contained a pearl.
I pictured my life revolving around her like
she was the world.
Her blush couldn't mask her blushing from
the way I look at her.
Her hair fell not so short of her shoulders;
she had it in a bob.

I wanted to weave through the cliffs her
thighs possessed and floor my vehicle into
her chest.
She would feel a rush of adrenaline,
steaming the turbines of her body to bind
her me.
I had to stop fantasizing and go open her
door.
From there, we were off to the restaurant. I
opened the door and she created a scene.
Her heels filed appeals to be tried for
murdering every girl in the room.
I pulled out her chair, and we sat.
The night was filled with leisure
conversation by candlelight. The
interlocking of our hands began to kindle a
flame that I hoped would never burn out.
We talked the night away until the waiter
told us it was closing time.
The ride back to her place made my heart
race against my brain.
I was going insane as I contemplate will I
make a move or not.
I got out and opened her door.
As we walked to her door, holding hands,
my heart began to beat faster.
My voice is up tempo as we go to say
goodbye.
She goes to open her door.
It's now or never.
I pull her back for more.
She looked confused, but then our lips
fused.
It was electrifying to embrace her.
I pulled away after about a minute to assess

her look. She appeared calm, but it was hard
to decipher.
She came and passionately kissed me.
From there, we were going back and forth
like we were in a cypher.
Her lips were punch lines that counter acted
mine every time.
The interlocking of our lips made sparks fly.
She stopped with a look and she told me to
come inside.
I felt like Halley's Comet was leaving a
comment on the face of the moon, because
we're only 20 with an old love like we're 61.
I wonder where we will be in 2061.
Hopefully we can witness the comet come
again as sparks fly between us going up the
stairs.
This is Heaven's stairway.
She stares waiting for me to come into her
room.
I proceed followed the procession of beauty
behind me closing the door.
Anticipation builds for what is in store.

Midnight Fire

Nicole and I are opposite sides of a magnet
attracting each other.
When we connect, we generate a magnetic
field strong enough to reverse the polarity of
Earth's poles.
She loves when I go south making her
tropical climate pour pools of rain.
My brain never grasped the idea of us being
intimate on this level.
Her black dress can't contain her curvaceous
frame.
I've always pictured her body as a canvas;
I stroke each corner gently for hours until a
Picasso was created.
She burned candles that are placed in the
four corners of this globe.
Anticipation builds below my belt from
wanting to get inside her world exploring
north and going Deep South.
Shadows arise from the melting wax forming
figures that dance along the walls.
I feel we are preparing to redefine Newton's
Laws of Motion as butterflies arise from the
primal desire in her eyes.
This artist has already sketched out her
intentions with me as I am drawn to her,
when she tells me come closer.
We're face to face with each other, eyes
locked on their verified targets.
The fire between us is sparked with the
interlocking of our lips, and it spreads
through our hands incinerating each other's

terrain.

This bed is a ring. She has met her match.

I intend to prove that I can be her champion
as she removes my belt.

She sits me on the bed and she pounces
wrapping her paws around.

Her tongue dances up my neck and her
fangs gently graze my ear.

My hands ride around her waist to the base
of her spine, up her back to pull her hair.

Her body was at rest until I applied my force
to put her prowess into motion.

Intimacy is all we are breathing as I enter her
slowly.

Her giggles from my aggression turn into
moans.

Her nails are daggers so I can go deeper,
because she wants some more of me.

Her top off, but I'm clocking in.

I'm working her for hours with a quick
lunch break in between shifts.

I love dining in.

I'm widening her eyes from the accelerated
penetration between her thighs;

I read her body language and then
capitalized the D.

She is deep.

I am hard.

I tease her by only giving her a teaser to the
end of a long story since she likes playing
with my head.

She's getting all of me and I'm receiving her
in a way I never thought I would see.

For every opposite action is a reaction, so I
increase and decrease the speed to satisfy

her every need.
We do it like we're in high school and her
mom just got home, so she wants me to
sneak through the back.
The bite of her bottom lip indicates she
loves it like that, but her arch is a gateway to
bridge me closer to her resolution.
We resolve all possible speculation to the
murder wrote on her walls.
They hold stories of a beast that feast on her
fruit she couldn't help but face the truth,
even though it made her choke.
We were drenched in sweat as the bed was
an ocean with depths full of conversation.
I look at her laying there.
She is shrouded in fatigue as she desperately
tries to find breath to recapture, but her
spirit was caught in the rapture of ecstasy
leaving this empty shell trembling.
My arms wrap around her body and we lie
there in the silence.
Golden flames gyrate on top of the melting
wax, possibly molding what a future with
Nicole may hold.

To What May Come

At one point I figured, if I never had her,
she would be impossible to lose.
I always thought about planning a move to
her mind set, and settling down in her
subconscious under the right circumstances.
I often imagined journeying through her
cerebral cortex and through the
hypothalamus, because I only want to be in
the cerebellum and any fears she may have,
get rid of them.
I thought of being her spine until she makes
me get off, because I'm getting on her
nerves.
That is what happens in most couple right?
We fuss and fight only to make up and blush
her face when we make love that night.
I pictured us painting portraits that portray
how much we care for each other through
the stroke of her anatomy.
I hope that happens regularly.
Maybe Monday through Friday.
We create new works of art on the weekend.
We have something planned for each other
at every week's end.
We graduate college.
She has dreams of giving back to the
community, so I would sponsor it.
We have our own type of business firm.
She clocks in my business and I give her
desk work in between shifts.
I bring flowers to her job and chocolates on
the holidays. We visit each other's family
through the holidays.

We plan vacations in May through July.
We have long walks on the beach and talk
about how fast time went by, and it brought
us here.
We go there.
We don't make moments.
We make monuments.
Every second we spend becomes
monumental by the hour, and I hope it
never changes.
We will go on dinner dates that are candle
lit.
Her expressions shine brighter than the
flames as I unveil my passion for her on one
knee.
I want to be her everything and more.
The one that makes her smile.
The one that will be her shield.
The one that will doctor her until she is
healed.
The only one that will provide resuscitation
to our love if it ever ceases to have life.
This is my word, which I will present to her
at her throne.
With her consent, we can be wealthier than
the richest man ever known.
Let's make a bed and nourish the sheets with
our nutrients until it sprouts a baby.
If she wants to go there, maybe.
If so, lets us work as a unit until he or she is
fully trained to be deployed out into the
world.
Our little E-3 will excel as they become a
specialist specializing in overcoming the
IED's that bombard their life.

Our child is a tank ready to fire an RPG at
any obstacle in their way.
Our kids' future will be major as we drill it
into their heads that they are captains.
Everyone they influence will be in their
company.
The more loyal friends they gain will
command everyone's attention.
Once the kids are out the house, Nicole and
I will enjoy our last few years.
They might bring us to tears, but we will
rewind the moments in life by visiting the
monuments we created.
Those will last.
We could grow old together knowing we
came first in our lives after God.
Maybe I'm thinking too far ahead, or maybe
I'm tangled in her comfort.
Nicole needs to come forth and let me know
where we headed from here.
I don't want to give all of me and she
provides me a quarter.
Maybe I am over thinking, but I really hope
things don't change.

It Wasn't Me

If naked people have no influence in society,
I will strip apart every fiber of my being
down to the strains of DNA to display a
gene.
Showing what I am meant to be as a man is
defined by a woman.
Finally, I have a girl to cherish.
I am her knight in the golden armor on a
chariot, dawned by horse that appears
celestial.
God displays our love to nations along the
celestial plane through constellations and
comets, but people hate to see one happy so
we are bombarded with comments.
Words from our peers are snakes that slither
into her ear. They travel along her thought
process and inject their venom until she
process doubt.
She has doubt in me.
She has doubt in us.
More occasions we fuss and argue about
nonsense.
I can sense she's allowing outside voices to
come in our home and vandalize the love we
treasure.
I stand my ground, but I can tell our
foundation is beginning to crack and ripple.
Rumors began to spread like ripples
throughout the water of our love.
They turned the tides against me.
I come home to tidal waves of accusations
that seem to topple most of the evening.
Why I'm just coming home?

Where have I been?
Who was it with?
What's the name of the "B", itching my last
nerve for her to think I would lay with dogs?
She has everything I do in increments to
incriminate me of cheating.
She insists on seeing my phone.
She is confident she will find some evidence
to convict and sentence me to a life without
her.
All I do is assure her, and she follows by
asking me if I'm sure. I chastise her about
her insecurity.
Her finger is the trigger pointed above the
shoulder; she's shooting headshots.
Her mouth is a Gatling gun unloading
multiple clips tearing through the flesh of
my ear making me feel inferior.
She wants to know the truth, yet still insist
that I'm lying.
She wants to know why I'm so quiet.
What is it I'm hiding?
These rumors aren't true.
She is being fed lies.
Nicole's friends are the reason our love is
meeting an untimely demise.
It shouldn't be about what he or she say.
It's about what we say, because we're the
ones running this show.
This sitcom doesn't require actors, so
directly cut them off.
She wanted to know why they would say
those things if it isn't true.
People don't like to see one doing better.
Everything they do is a script to scribe false

hieroglyphs into her walls, because she's so
easily molded into believing its true.
Dismiss the cases brought against me,
because I am innocent.
I'm tired of coming to a home that is a court
room and a girlfriend who's a judge.
The gavel she throws at me is opinions of
her peers attempting to be signed into law,
but those accusations are immediately
vetoed, because it's disrupting the order in
my home.

Paved Cement

I wish concrete wouldn't get hard once
mixed with water.
I wish it could just stay wet gravel, but roads
would sink for everyone attempting to travel
so no one would get anywhere.
Sometimes, I feel like me and Nicole aren't
getting anywhere.
This place in our lives is a four by four
cubicle with walls that forever elongate
inhibiting us from climbing out.
We shout like apes swinging from vines that
dangle from trees; all attributes that were
humanly possible became primal.
The house became civil war because she was
the south and seceded from our union.
She still is enslaved to the outside thoughts
and opinions that was slowly becoming her
noose, choking the life out of the kindred
spirit I once knew.
That pain in the back of my neck was the
rope's tension. This ten shuns me out of
parts of her that are vital.
Signs show me the heartbeat that pumped
the blood through this relationship is fading.
I am the EKG.
I feel like she's slowly slipping away.
This engagement ring is the octagon
containing multiple rounds of our ultimate
fighting.
These constant heavy weight bouts sprawl
into doubt after each match. Flames are
sparked as a blitzkrieg of "F" bombs and "I
hate you" are dropped sending our sanctuary

a blaze.

I threaten to leave and she appears
completely un-phased. We are off to our
corners of the house and she feels third
world.

I am an A10 flying over to drop a care
package hoping it would save our invisible
children.

I don't want her stress to be the Joseph
Kony.

Hold me.

She doesn't want to be let go.

I'm here for her she should know.

I say, "I love you".

She says, "You too".

We look at each other then head to the
room.

However, make up sex can't mask the fact
that our relationship needs refining.

Right after we are back to square one.

We have sex then back to arguing when
we're done.

I feel our separation from the church has us
in this state. How can I say I love her, and
our relationship is no longer based around
our faith?

I thought we were supreme, until I was left
to cover the court cost.

A cliché was her verdict.

It's not you, it's me.

I was charged with being too giving and she
hoped I would change.

She regrets the time spent, because to this
dime, I was a copper Lincoln.

All along, another guy I been kissing.

Her judgment was to explore her options
and select one whose game is unpredictable.
She became the soil to a seed that wasn't
mine.
During sex, it was his name she wanted to
glorify.
I see why she stopped going to church,
because this other guy became her god.
He became her messiah while I tried to take
her higher so we are on an even plane.
My feelings were unconscious pilots heading
into the twin towers on 9/11.
I need to dial 9 1 1.
I'm in need of a medic, but medical
procedure can't proceed me past this
comfortable lie.
At that moment, I died on the inside.

Missing Pieces

The lights are off; the dark actually provides
some comfort to my distraught heart.
The shadows hold photographs of my
expressions after she told me.
These four walls are painted with my
emotions.
There's no more in the can.
The spots not covered were painted with my
fist.
Just thought of it connecting with Nicole's
face gave me a sense of bliss, but all my
senses are dead nerve endings that can't
make sense of why I got treated like this.
I feel crushed under a mountain of my
emotions that won't ever become dew.
My emotions are airborne allergens caused
by heartbreak that contaminate my
proximity.
I been given a few weeks to live
approximately, which I will use to tell that
chick to kick rocks.
It's too late.
She walked away after stoning me to death.
My last words are used to try to persuade
her.
She purred for another man on suede sheets.
I try to piece together a puzzle that will
never be completed.
Each one of these rooms are beasts that
consume me.
It was all a game and she was ready with her
poker face.
I was dealt a hand of jacks since I was her

perfect ass.
She refused to be my queen even though I
was a committed King.
She jacked my trust and traded all that for an
ace that fit perfectly in her hole.
Solitary is my state.
Her act was a chainsaw that made a
massacre of my heart as she moved with her
new man to Texas.
My eyes refuse to be clear.
I try to get in contact as I polish the lens of
my scope to help me cope with feeling dead.
Rounds of my hatred are cocked and loaded
by the multiple.
Times I wanted to shoot her subtracting her
soul from her flesh.
Adding mutilation by cutting off her limbs
and breast as I would wait for the cops to
come and place me under arrest.
I could strap her to the bed she
consummated her cheating ways.
The kitchen would be set ablaze for every
room that contained memories.
Burn her body to a crisp for playing with me
like this, because my feelings were a game.
That would be checkmate.
As for the guy, I would place a bullet in his
head then completely unload my steel.
Maybe I would feel better.
I'll check them off my murder list.
Let her rest with her mate.
Could this really be my fate?
Why should it be?
I prayed for us to be grounded and well
rooted, but her action was a blade that

sawed my tree.
I seek where we went wrong, but all it does
is hide. I fell down a chasm of deaf while I
poured out my insides. This whole time,
have I been alone?
Was it all really worth it?
I provided a relationship worth a Benjamin,
but no button could fasten the loose ends
that could bring about change.
I'm curious to know her motives.
I use to believe our souls were tide in the
bountiful wonders of the seven that already
existed.
Apart of me is loss; place on the back of
milk cartons because it can't be found.
Has anyone seen me?
She showed me another side of love other
than the sun.
I am shrouded in the darkness of deceit.
My heart is offered at the altar for demons
to devour, altering my perceptive my mind.
I am cold-hearted.
That thermonuclear rush no longer drives
my reactor, because I am cold.

She

She.

Nicole.

Fall into a chasm of the broken promises
you made.

Maybe the faults will reveal the lines she
crossed, and the earthquake will rupture the
foundation of her new found land.

Let that quake be a 9.9 on the Richter scale
as she weights the options of being faced
with life and death.

Let that quake make a tsunami that drowns
her in the depths of her deceit.

I said, "Let that quake make a tsunami that
drowns her in the depths of her deceit."

That is what she gets for cheating on me.

Allow her hands to cling to her throat as she
desperately tries to purchase some air.

I brought her a ring.

I had intentions of making her my wife.

I wouldn't buy her life.

Spike her cup.

She'd drink it up.

Wake up in a desert with no resources for
claiming to know love.

The water ran dry from the lie she sprung.

She has dry mouth because she's incapable
of speaking anything else from her tongue.

I feel robotic like I'm in a trance.

Vaginal mesh couldn't seal the snakes that
crept from her thighs.

White lies secrete from the lips that appear
so innocent in her eyes. She is walking down

the streets naked.
Beware this premature fetus that calls herself
woman. She is missing some brain tissue.
Use them to wipe the tears from those
pitiful eyes when the new man leaves. Cry a
river that stretches as long as the Mississippi.
Drown in its current. She is exposed. She is
rags of what she once was. No needle and
thread could stitch this bitch into an article
of clothing worth being worn. She feels torn
apart, but she wouldn't know the half.
That part of you is burning alive so good
luck finding yourself.
Unplug the EKG. Let's see how long her
eyes remain open with her TV missing.
She is a soul being withheld during the
tribulation.
She is a fallen star spangled with the banner
of adultery so she is satin.
Freedom will ring when the world is free of
this beast.
To think, I thought she was once a beauty.
I perceived her to be a queen.
I vowed to never let anything or anyone
come in between us.
Some may say I'm being bitter, but how can
I be blamed when I was use to everything
being sweet?
She shifted gears when I thought our cruise
was under control.
Even though she parked me in unfamiliar
spot, she is still driving me insane.
Its whatever.
I'm far from good, and even further from
better.

However, no amount lace fronts could tie
my shoes to make me run back to her.
Those fronts did make me cold.
Now because of her, my attitude will be to
scold every woman that comes next.
It's a shame that the following girl will suffer
from the actions dealt to me by my ex.

Comfort

By: Lemarcus Jackson

Are we ever 100% comfortable?
Feelings of insecurity, thinking we have
hidden our impurities.
That thought still pops in our heads, "What
if someone finds out?"
Can you really guarantee without a doubt
that no one knows but you and God?
I searched for my comfort in many forms,
shapes and sizes, finding women in disguises
pretending to be that comfort that I need;
but all they did was succeed in stripping
away my already abused trust for a moment
of lust, not caring about my feelings.
As a man we are told never become
vulnerable species.
I long for the strength to cut my emotions
off at times.
Then I turned to my writings for my
comfort, bleeding emotions into a
manuscript but my mind is tripped how I
could open up to a blank page.
Yet my voice feels caged inside my throat
when it comes to expressing my discomfort
with my imperfections.
Comfort, free of worry from the things of
this world.
A longing to be protected and connected to
someone or something.
I think babies are the only people who truly
feel it without having a worry in the world.
I want that comfort. I long for it.

Hour Glass

Life plays too many games.
I feel like I'm on extended pause without
knowing if I will be restarted or subjected to
a game over.
I'm sitting in the window.
We both staring at each other.
We can't stand the sight of one another.
He pretends to be me and I see through
him.
His hopeful eyes eventually grows dim and
becomes dark.
He is cold.
His temperature drops, and this is every day.
In the morning when I see him he is bright
and full of optimism.
He is ready to seize the day.
He's ready to take over.
He's plotting as we speak.
Yet, he never talks back.
I ask what will happen tomorrow and he
mouths my words.
I tell him better days will come and he gives
the same reassurance.
However, I wonder how can he insure that
chance?
This window is a hypocrite.
Through him, I appear bright but its only
for limited hours.
The times change.
I need more to spend.
How can a man be faithful to something
that he's not currently seeing?
Where is the believing?

I feel trapped behind this glass of emotion
as I'm being pulled deeper beneath the grain.
I finally realize something.
I am the sand waiting to see some change,
but I'm just sitting here accumulating more
hope to get out from behind this stained
glass and see my dreams instead of my own
reflection.
This glass is stained.
No matter how much polish is applied it'll
eventually go back to its original state. I
don't want to move there. I just want to be
home, but where is home if this world is
every man for their own?
How can I believe in change when time is
spent being the same?

Treasure Chess

Candace was always told that she is a queen.
Her body is a temple.
Her life is precious and not to let any man
enter her unless he presented the key to her
heart.
That key not only unlocked her greatest
treasure, but he solved the labyrinth in her
mind.
See, Candace was a maze yet, such an
amazing person with a kindred spirit.
She uplifted everyone she came in contact
with.
She was available when help would call.
She trusted everyone and was forgiving to
those that did her wrong, but that was just
the type of person she was.
She was a daddy's girl.
He always would bounce her on his lap.
She was young so she was oblivious to the
meaning of the words "night cap".
All she knew was not to say a word, because
daddy was going to give her a treat.
The minutes were murder and an innocent
heart no longer had a beat.
Candace gasped from the pain.
The words, "night" and "cap" will always be
seared into her pain.
The knight was daddy's horse that she had
stoke.
Daddy's cap braided through her like a filter
that almost made her choke.
The way daddy touched her she thought it
was love. She didn't know any better.

After the crime was committed, the word
"love" he would never tell her.
She no longer had her prized possession.
Daddy stolen her treasure repeatedly after he
would say, "Take a deep breath because you
might feel it in your chest."
Candace was a pawn to someone she
thought was a king.
Her jewels no longer glowed.
Her pearls bled from the destruction of her
hymen.
Her walls carried memories of the murder
daddy wrote on her insides.
She was too young to understand the act,
but daddy would always have it staged.
He would dress her up in her favorite dress.
He would even do her hair.
They would go to mommy and daddy room
and he would say, "We got some secrets to
share."
With no care, little Candace went along.
Daddy would manipulate her by singing her
favorite song.
"I'm a little tea cup; short and stout.
Here is my handle ; here is my spout."
He taught her how to please a man before
she knew what fellatio was.
Her London bridge was torn down and all
she could do was look at the face of Big Ben
counting the minutes.
Now grown up she can't give herself to a
man and it's all because she doesn't know
love.
A man's touch makes her skin crawl.
She doesn't let them touch her inside.

Even if that isn't their intention, she sees
man and only see the multiple times daddy
lied.
He pirated her treasure.
She feels worthless; all her valuables were
looted from her chest.
She can't let go of his transgressions that are
scribed on her breast.
Candace no longer believes in fairytales.
Her childhood died that night in Daddy's
sheets.
She was so wide spread.
Her labyrinth walls are a tomb to house the
part of her that is dead.

My Baby

You have such big eyes.
When I look into them I see pools.
Your eyes are pools that I want to dive into
and swim to the deepest depths of your soul
until the weight of your heart dissolves me
into dust.
As soil, allow me to be planted into your
soul so I can sprout and grow as one with
you.
When my branches are strong enough, they
will protrude through your chest cavity to fill
any holes you may have.
They will rest underneath your heart.
They are there to provide support for
whenever life comes at you on a large scale
and begins to weigh you down.
I will keep you level.
My roots will travel through your
bloodstream providing you nutrients such as
iron, carbon, and zinc.
I need to keep you healthy, because you are
a precious metal that I hope to preserve and
treasure.
The laws of physics won't physically be able
to explain how two people walk as one
body.
I hold you inside of me.
I carry your spirit.
I want to write every letter of the alphabet
on your spine until the monotonousness
gets on your nerves.
I want to touch you in ways that puts our
heart rate in synchronous motion.

As well as rewrite the dictionary, because it
doesn't possess enough words to describe or
define my devotion to you.
I want my kiss to inject my feelings into your
veins causing them to expand into cylinders.
I want to be 360 with you, but still come at
you at the right angle.
No matter which curves come our way, our
ends will still be connected.
I want to conquer every part of your mind
like I'm Napoleon Bonaparte.
I want to take your bones apart and infuse
with them, because I always pictured be a
part of your frame.
I will be the ribs that protect your heart.
I'll be your genetic makeup just so I can
wear everything that makes you on my face.
When people see me, they'll immediately see
you.
I'll be your tree as the sun is absorbed into
your beautiful skin.
From there, undergo photosynthesis to
provide you the oxygen you need for life.
Can you picture that?
Each of our moments together is a photo
synthesized in scrapbooks.
We can reminisce about past experience.
Understand, I want to nurture and care for
you, because you are my baby.

Museum

I always wondered would I be remembered
once I pass on.
I want to be remembered.
I don't want to be remember for just be the
person that I was, but I want every action I
committed to be archived.
They could be different exhibits displaying
different aspects of my life.
The baby exhibit exhibits my early years,
before I even learned how to crawl,
progressing into my toddler years when I
began to run my mother up a wall.
I swear I thought she was Spiderman.
A wax figurine of me in the cabinets making
music with the pots and pans.
That noise my mother could not stand.
She'd smack me on the hand and I'll cry into
my kid years where trouble was my best
friend.
We would go into the situations together,
but I would always be the only one getting
the whooping.
Every lash would whip up a twister turning
into my teens.
Hormones running rapid when these girls
began to develop.
Feeling began to envelop as I carelessly
passed them on from female to female.
It progressed until all those feelings were
expressed in their sheets with my emotions
flushed in the rubber.
They wanted me to be their man, but I could
never bring myself to make cither one of

them my lover.
The college exhibit would be broken down
into different stages.
I acted hard my first semester.
I portrayed many faces.
Intoxicated from partying too much I would
wake up in some unexplainable places.
That's my own fault.
I was smart even to know which lines not to
cross, but I didn't use common sense.
That was when I needed to change.
Six months of training, the boy is becoming
a man.
The drill sergeants engraved it into my mind
that there is no "I can't", only thing that
exist is "I can."
Dress that figurine with army fatigues, but
people still wouldn't feel what I went
through.
Onto the next segment when I finally found
someone true.
She is amazing even though I was too blind
at first.
She followed me from the beginning, and
was willing to accept me at my worse.
Now she makes me feel like the best.
We already making plans.
A couple exchanges of vows and if time
allows hopefully we will start a family.
Then in later years, enjoy the last few we
have left.
When God calls us home, comfortably we
will rest.
At the end of the tour, it'll be concrete
statues of us holding hands.

It'll be like we are frozen in time.
The other displays may melt, but the feelings
from those moments will always be felt.
The feeling is real, it can almost be touched.
Cherish everything and everyone while they
are here.
Everyone and moment has meaning.
I don't know about everyone else, but I'd
rather be memorable than just a memory.

Ocean Eyes

Sometimes I dream of drowning and right
before I hit the water I wake up in a cold
sweat.
That's how it is when it comes to loving
someone.
The water looked shallow so I decided to
dive in, but I miscalculated its actual depth.
Now I find myself trying to swim to shore,
but her relentless tides keep pulling me
further apart from her.
Her current is aggressive, and constantly it
pulls me down.
She has high tide hopes that I will one day
drown in her, but I still put up a fight to stay
afloat.
I am not the one you should give
unconditional love to, because I am afraid of
pouring my all into one body.
I can't bring myself to tell her, because I
wouldn't want to see her sink.
I wouldn't want to watch her crash under
my truthful waves.
I am calm, but I am drenched in the fear
that covers the face of my Earth.
I am scared to make any girl my world,
because I don't want to get pulled fathoms
below their leagues.
I'm not the type to compete for a woman
and my main goal isn't to only make her wet.
Although, I want to drown her mind in the
scorching ideology of what we can be, that is
guaranteed to make her sweat.
I have my moments when my temper will

boil, and my feelings will appear to
evaporate.

I may become a gas, but if she just allows
me to be who I am I promise to always be
solid.

I one day hope to become liquefied or a
H_2O molecule in her ocean.

Maybe we can become compounds and
serve a sentence locked within each other.

I hope one day I can behold light beyond
her surface, but the fathoms are where
shadows lie and that's all I see.

If her tsunamis crash land, I could be the
one to pull her from the rubble.

She could be that one to create a ripple that
parts my ways, so I may allow her to come
through, but that's just wishful thinking.

I'm sorry for being so shallow.

9-1-1

Nowadays love is an impatient patient going
through outpatient surgery because we allow
outside doctors to operate on this heart
failing relationship.
Our cardiac was under arrest to each other's
task force.
These outside doctors not certified, but
attempt to give a diagnosis which forced this
task at hand.
We don't touch each other the same.
The body of our relationship is failing and
no part is trying to be blamed.
The timing is bad.
Its hands are crooked.
More time should have went to planning this
trip before we booked it.
This relationship is illiterate since we
struggle trying to read each other.
We try to find ourselves and allow our
partners to go missing.
We don't know our partner like the back of
our hand and claiming to be in love.
One problem arises and we file for
separation.
No one wanting the title, but use love
loosely just to feel the sensation.
Sending Satin into the ears of those who
truly is trying to feel.
That lie eventually reveals its poker face and
then we sit and ask ourselves, "What's the
deal?" We are blinded by the portrayal of
love on the TV.
Love & Hip Hop is lust beating to the

melody of misery that will eventually stop.
The Real Housewives don't deserve the role.
I bet if casted into a real setting, they
wouldn't have a clue how to build a home.
Television tells us visions of false love that
we see.
The falsification pools into the streams of
our mind preventing us from diving into the
vast ocean of real love.
The reality of love nowadays is just a show
to get a few ratings in the public eye.
Open your iris treat love as your pupil.
Raising it right so it can grow and maybe
touch others, because right now it is dying.
It's the only one of its kind.
Provide shock therapy to this shocking
therapeutic lie.
The ambulance came late.
Doctors can no longer operate with no
reliable option.
Cremate love.
Now it's just dust like the rest of us.

Self Portrait

I begin to draw this picture of myself from
how I see me seeing the person looking back
in the mirror, because he is drawing what
resides in my soul which is not visible to the
naked eye.
Looking at him, I grab this pen bleeding its
ink onto this white page until the lines
contour a face of young age.
It is youthful.
Life is embedded, but it's too alive to appear
restless.
The forehead is a forecast for a storm of
vast knowledge by this projection.
It's full of entry ways and blockades from
paths not accessible by just anyone;
My pen digs deep into its soil to find that
this is deeply rooted.
This is filled with the essence of herbs that
shower from the sky to make it's hair
radiant.
From the hair down to private areas of
forbidden fruit, my pen depicts branches
that reach from the heart to touch others.
The chest contains treasure beneath the
breast that beats life into whatever it may
kiss.
The lips are pink rose petals blown off its
but to expose thorns.
Every beauty needs protection.
They come apart from the stem to reveal
who it is, but my pen depicts these eyes,
these beautiful brown eyes untainted by lies
yet stained with unrequited love with the

hope shimmering behind their lens.
I can see it clearly.
This picture possesses a delicate touch and
soft skin.
So I gently graze my hand across its face,
and both of our hearts begin to race with
neither trying to get ahead of the other.
I am free to riffle through its pages.
This caricature's sexual prowess is amazing
as red ink can't mask or deoxidize the blaze
burning between us once I'm inside this
caricature's arm, under its garments,
exploring every segment of its figure to lay
files into its cabinet with multiple
compartments.
This feels right.
I look down at this page out of breath,
because I just poured out all the talent I had
left into me on this page.
I was trying to find myself, but this drawing
already knew my location.
I was too blind to realize this girl was already
mine before she even said yes.
I was too oblivious.
She saw something in me that I didn't see in
myself until I put her on paper.
I sketched the inner me and she was drawn
to that.

If This World Were Mine

Every day of the week would be
commemorated for each milestone in our
life together.
It would archive the first time I met you at
hello, to the point where I made you my
Mrs.; it would be a national holiday.
The word of our love would spread to
nations worldwide, because baby girl you
too precious of a lady to hide, inside.
See baby, if this world were mine...Luther
can keep the birds and the bees, because all
your hopes and dreams would be places at
your feet without any fees.
I get on my knees to thank the Lord every
day for blessing me with an angel of your
caliber.
If this world were mine...no diamond ring
would signify my love for you.
Instead, each feeling for you would manifest
into and image that would regress to every
memory that we created projected into the
night sky.
You will love star gazing.
Constellations will constantly tell stories of
us for future generations.
If this world were mine...no other woman
would be allowed to degrade such a fine
name.
They would be minute and all their talk
would be on mute.
We would be channeled into each other as
storms would turn to their eyes and tell
them, "Keep Calm".

Date a poet and you'll live forever, because
my words will embody your spirit.
If this world were mine...heartache would be
an unknown emotion, because this love I'm
giving you possesses unwavering trust and
devotion.
That is all I'm willing to provide.
I'll be your mate if you provide me the soul.
I'll wage war to be compensated with your
right hand.
I am a lefty.
You may be a Libra, but by the scale of our
affection, I'm sure we will balance out.
If this world were mine...I would twist reality
so every day we're together would be a new
experience.
Every hour you're on this earth you'll be
living any fantasy.
If this world were mine...we would make
love in the most exotic locations, filled with
so much of our sexual imaginations.
It would be untamed and uncut.
The National Geographic would label them
as the new 7 world wonders.
You wouldn't have to wander the world
searching for that lucky one.
If This World Were Mine...no ailment would
harm that precious body you possess.
I confess, I'll fight that disease off with the
two hands god gave me.
If This World Were Mine...would make
everything I said in this poem true.
I'll try my best to provide you with
something you're not use to.

Sheldon Gilton

That was the only time I felt like I matter,
but your actions took my mass and now the
only thing that occupies this space is
loneliness.
I guess I'll always expect be nobody.
I'm the nobody that only had value when my
face was buried in the pillow.
The nobody undeserving of a eulogy after
being buried six feet under you.
I'm the nobody that waits for you in tears
until they leave a permanent print, because
you can't break something further that
possesses a splint.
The nobody that wishes for you to come
around or ricochet just so your balls can
bounce off my walls, but this is not pinball.
The nobody that reopens her legs expecting
you to open her heart, however, these legs
are a guillotine that would decapitate the
same head you use to rape me.
I'm the nobody that asks, "Why", but is only
greeted with "because". I would saw off
every part of you used to manipulate me
then broadcast the gore like it's the latest
buzz. The nobody whose eyes once
possessed an abundance of hope.
Now they are only in a drought because no
more tears run for you since I refuse to be
nobody.

on the inside, but now I am "Being Mary Jane".

I wanted you to catch the contact so we could get high, but you used a kiss to ignite the ends of my buds and my heart slowly burned to ashes from the lies.

You own my tear ducts and every drop they release.

I gave my all on a silver platter and sat there starving for a piece.

Why my love was the only one that came, and yours could never come?

Why "maybes" were left to keep me company while I could never be secured by, what will get done?

I guess I'll always be that worthless trophy on the shelf collecting dust.

I'm the girl that can't be treasured for her mind and heart, because she's only good for a midnight bust.

I'm the one that calls you baby, but can't be nurtured like one.

The one that is shown at the time of the setting sun, because that was the only time you took me out.

You did your dirt during the day.

You're unable to give yourself to her because you're thinking of me; the essence of you is left in my sheets and that was the only time you said, "Nicole, you complete me."

That was the only time I felt whole.

Off With His Head

If you wasn't real, why did you treat me like
I was a good catch?
I am stagnant water in a bucket occupied
with spores of his mosquitos that grew to
drink the life out of me.
I was his Petri dish for lies to mature and
cultivate my mind, which forced my legs
open for this bloodsucker to enter my body.
You would sex me and then hang me in the
closet.
Later that night, take me out like I'm a
homosexual, but all I wanted was you to feel
the same instead of our home, oh so sexual.
The first one lead to two, and after three I'm
thrown in the hamper four you to return.
I'm just the girl that has seen through you
but still got casted in your play.
The girl whose thoughts were directed to
her being a ten until you took five.
I don't feel alive.
You make me feel like a ghost in a shell
trying to find a home, but the only person
she meets is a person named Alone.
My heart was a loan that did not get paid.
What I thought was 50 Shades of Gray
turned out to be black and white.
We don't mix.
Countless night I waited up for you while
you were out soiling these other chicks.
See I'm more than just a "man's best friend"
that walks on a leash by your side.
I was the one that provided a lavished home

You're in another woman now.
This is the end.

only thing you expanded was my walls.
I was wet.
You made them warp.
The rain came after you left, I didn't have a
tarp.
A part of me died when I crucified my
morals, but I still didn't learn the lesson
since I'm wishing he would return.
I caught you first.
Why you had to go off and get traded?
I never thought I could make it without you,
so now what do I do?
I feel detached from this world.
I'm ready to be raptured.
Lord, remove this captured heart so it may
no longer beat.
My staff possesses no notes.
I can't even be in tuned with someone else
when I possess no tone.
I am alone.
I am empty.
Tears can no longer run.
My words can't dive off my tongue into
someone's ear when nobody is here.
I am alone.
Depression is my company.
I am a ship that thought she found her
captain, but he's intoxicated by Morgan.
If I could afford more guns, I would kill
them both.
Your act severed my air.
I am about to drop.
Why did you cause this abrupt stop, when
we were just about to begin?

Face Value

If I put all my dreams into body art, would it
be able to catch the essence of what we had?
The ink is in the second layer of my skin.
You are imprinted on my body.
My legs were the book and my vagina was
the place holder for you to pick up where
you left off.
I continued to read us for what we appeared
to be.
Your cover was intricate.
For so long I read between the lines and saw
you for what you were, but I could not put
an end to it, period.
Your words bled through my pages.
You made me weak.
This unsettling feeling traveled through my
nerves until it reached the pores of my feet.
The ground seemed to shake.
I accepted all your faults.
You crossed too many lines, and sometimes
I couldn't even have an appetite.
You were my fill.
Yet, you only parked in my lot when it was
convenient and left saying, "I'll be back"
when you know you never really meant it.
That's all I was to you...just a parking space.
I thought I really drove you crazy when all
along you was just down for the drag race.
Beginning at my thighs to finish at my heart,
and sometimes you didn't back up, you
would just have your genitals in park.
I gave you brain, but to my knowledge the

strike his frontal lobe.

I run back to the room and turn on all of the lights.

He wakes up startled while trying to hold my wrist, because I am ready to fight.

Boxers with lipstick on the front.

So this chick been sucking?

I guess the experience with me wasn't satisfying.

Is it that bad in our home that he had to go outside to get some loving?

My face is red.

My emotions are about to blow.

All it takes is for him to say the wrong thing and I am going to explode.

He stood in silence, but in my eyes he was not golden.

He said he no longer loved me, and with those words my heart broken.

He just didn't know how to break it to me.

He never wanted to hurt me.

He was planning to keep it in the dark so I would not have to worry.

His hours of making bread ended around
five,
but he takes an extra six and comes home
around eleven.
Why when I question his whereabouts, he
always responds with, "I was by Kevin."
I never met him before.
Is he more important than me?
How can I not feel insecure when the man I
love is always disappearing?
He blinds me with a dollar camouflaged in
lies so I don't see his change.
A lot of men do this and it doesn't make
sense.
Some will destroy house and home for a
quick opportunity then wonder why they are
alone.
I feel he wants variety.
He doesn't touch me the same.
The look in his eyes are reptilian.
His aura is no longer sincere; I feel like I've
been sleeping with a chameleon.
I don't go to sleep high off him and this bed
doesn't feel like mine.
The fear of him with another woman creeps
up my spine.
I am nervous.
While he is sleep, I find a condom missing
out the dresser.
Then underneath sofa pillows was his
boxers smudged in the red lipstick used to
dress her.
He been playing with my head.
I feel like I am about to go insane!
Emotions build up in my fist; I want to

One Eye Open

I spy deceit when I see it, but he would
never come out and confirm my suspicions.
I share a bed with a stranger.
I don't recognize this person.
The person who was once so loving, another
side of him appears to be emerging from the
depths of his soul.
I bathe in it.
The warm, comfortable temperature is
changing because maybe I've been in it too
long.
It's becoming cold.
He would say he loves me like I'm just
getting out the shower and he's standing
there with a towel to embrace me.
He would wrap me real tight and that made
us close knit.
We are stitched together.
I embody his body as my apparel so I wear
his heart on my sleeves.
His word was my heels that I trusted to help
me overcome any hill, because I walked by
faith and not by sight.
See, I had faith in him.
He loved me to steer me right when I
wanted to go left, and always retraced his
steps so I wouldn't be left questioning.
He was beautiful, but I feel my antique is
losing his value.
I'm trying to muster up trust, but how can I
when all his words sound like baloney?

I don't understand how a man can be this
good, or love a battered woman consumed
with so much insecurity.
I am too full off past experiences to even get
a bite of his love.
It's not him, it's me.
I should go apologize to him for diminishing
his character.
I leave the kitchen table with hope Brandon
and I could be equally sturdy.
I go to our room and he is in the shower.
I sit on the bed anxious for him to get out.
I'm going to give my man so much loving
while he's still soaked.
When we're done we'll be equally yoked in
each other's spirit and mind.
His phone starting to ring on the night
stand.
I answered it and darkness fell over me
where I stood.
I felt the reaper excavating my heart along
with every beat out my chest.
It was a female saying she could still feel
"HIM" beneath her breast.

What's his deal?
I refuse to be played.
Just something about him appears to be off,
but that look in his eyes always turn me on.
I find myself retracing his steps to find clues
to his infidelity.
I'm trying to magnify nothing into
something.
I am unsettled.
I feel like he is secretly embezzling all I got
to offer to provide it to another.
Yeah, that's exactly what it is.
How dare he try and play me for a fool, but
I already exposed this clown.
I should have known he was just looking for
a good time.
He is childish, and I'll be damn if I spend
my life trying to raise a man.
He doesn't value a woman.
He doesn't realize how rich he is, but wait,
maybe I am getting ahead of myself.
The man didn't do anything wrong.
He is always there when I am in need, and
he satisfies all my wants.
However, this ominous presents looms in
my head whenever we go to bed.
My dreams of us are free falling to only
crash hard.
I feel we are becoming detached.
I feel I am no longer his rib.
I feel our hearts aren't beating on the same
accord.
I wish I could just pause life and see things
for what it is instead of what I am expecting
it to be.

Boomerang

Wait, this seems too good to be true.
Brandon is just too perfect.
He does everything right, and I like that he
does, but I'm just waiting for him to go
wrong.
I am anticipating it in every action, in every
word.
I'm waiting for him to dig his own grave,
because I refuse to be treated like dirt.
I'm just ready to shovel him into the darkest
part of my mind, but he hasn't given me a
reason to bury him.
He doesn't treat me like garbage.
His words doesn't even smell like trash, and
I'm usually good at sensing the odor of a
liar.
He is consistent, never wavering.
He doesn't have any patterns, but I'm still
trying to shape him into something he isn't.
I need to stop drawing conclusions, but I'm
having a hard time believing this resolution
is the perfect image.
His words are genuine.
I am intoxicated.
His smile is sincere, but I only perceive sin
being seared into my brain.
It is blinding, almost spellbinding.
Yet, I still can't bring myself to dispel this
binding force he has over me. In my eyes,
our future is braille.
I'm blind to his hidden ambitions and our
path is bumpier than it's supposed to be.

He is breathtaking.
If he ever left physically, I would chase him
in my sleep.
This life we have is merely temporary, but I
know when my eyes are closed he'll always
be in my reach.
I can touch him.
I am embracing us.
He gives me so much adrenaline, but never
is the one to rush. He takes his time.
When we are together, everything appears to
be paused.
We play like we're kids even though we're
moving forward.
Let's fall asleep and runaway in our dreams
as we fast-forward to sixty-six.
I'm in route to him.
We ride with the top down, but I can't be
sad when every moment with him is
paradise.

His cerebral cortex is a support beam that
shines rays of hope into my eyes.
Optimism is all I see.
He is specially designed.
He is not only my lover, he is my best
friend.
It is not hard for him to express.
My tracks are railroads to my heart where his
emotions train me how to trust.
He would present me his hand just so I can
be wrapped and sealed in his arms.
I close my eyes to wake up in space.
Zodiac signs direct me to him.
We are galaxies that collide to create new
nebulas.
His love is like my body soaking in hot
water.
My pores are open for his follicles to enter.
He makes me feel like I am on a beach
watching the tide come and recede.
We are consistency and so easy to please.
I feel so free like my arms are wings and he
is the wind giving me the ability to fly.
My tears of joy are waterfalls that grow into
rivers.
He streams through the current to bring me
to an oasis.
The taste of our love is so sweet; the flavors
are plastered on our faces.
He is my lion and I am his lioness.
I dream of us lying in a nest of bouquets like
Adam and Eve.
Even with so much nature around us, the
oxygen in my body still manages to leave.

Paradise

He loves me.
Brandon does.
He loves me like the wind blowing against
hot skin.
He cools me down when I am heated.
The love he gives me is fire.
It strikes me.
It makes perfect sense that we are a perfect
match.
He loves me like freshly picked fruit that will
never rot.
He provides me with the trunk of the tree.
The stability required for us to branch out
and produce beautiful leaves.
He reassures that he will never leave or
change colors even when things begin to
fall.
He makes the dead winter in my heart come
alive.
He raises my temperature.
He makes me greet the sun rise.
He is the spring in my step.
He gives me new life despite the multiple
times I have wept.
He loves me like I'm witnessing heaven on
earth. I am raptured into his being.
We are one. He is my sun and I am his
moon.
He brings day to nights and I provide him
rest.
His heart is an open guideline with
instructions on how he intends to love me.

of you.
I love your taste.
You make my heart race.
I give you just as much and you throw it right back.
I'm thrown for a loop.
I enjoy revolving around your mind.
You relieve all my tension.
Your love is your wand; I am hypnotized so I can't help but pay attention.
You have me in a trance.
I love your every action.
You slid deep into the hole of my heart and love was my ending transaction.
Even though we desperately want to make love, you provide me something more.
You provide me with intimacy.

Boy teach me.

I am eager to learn.

Give me a few lessons.

I'll get it down with some practice.

The size of the work load does not matter

just as long as you get the job done.

I just adore all your effort.

Boy please me.

You make loving you so easy.

You drive me crazy.

You steer me in all the right directions.

You make me feel out my mind.

I'm deeply into you.

You open so many locked doors.

You make me willing and anxious for you to

come inside.

You make me feel high.

You take me to another level.

Any walls I had up, you patiently broke

them down with your chisel.

You make me feel sculpted. I cannot

possible think or grab letters to form words.

You make my heart flutter while giving me

butterflies.

Our hearts are opposite, but they combine

like contractions and they expand.

I find it hard to withstand so much love

being given to me all at once.

I never had it this good before.

I crave more.

I don't want you to stop.

You rise to the occasion and make me feel

like I'm on top, of everything.

This is important.

I give you a piece of me, in return, I get all

Spellbound

Brandon.
Your body is so breath taking.
I suffocate at the slightest touch.
My gasps desperately try to catch an ounce
of air when your lips hover over my neck.
You have my mind abducted.
Feel free to explore my mind.
You'd be amazed at all the wonders you will
find.
Disconnect the veins and link them with
yours so our minds will be connected.
So whatever you feel, I will taste.
Whatever you see, anticipation will be ready
for you to embrace.
My eyes are locked with yours as you ignite
me with your key.
Boy you turn me on.
Your touch sets fire to my skin.
The look in your eye makes me excited and I
never want this love to end.
Your hands slither across my frame.
Your soft whispers plant images in my head.
I can feel them grow.
You make me crave more.
You touch the deepest part of me, even
places that I had closed from you once
before.
The mix of your brush fuses our souls.
You nail the walls and both of our bodies
hold.
Your gentle strokes are precise as though
you're creating a masterpiece.

in them.
Maybe I would be able to understand your
walk of life and the baggage you had to
pocket."

You are so smooth.
I love the way you touch me.
Let us go to the room.

I'm liking you and you're obviously liking
me.
Out of all the things you could do, with me
right here is where you chose to be."
  You're right, I could be doing other things.
  I guess it's something about you that makes
               me curious.
Brandon: "You make me curious as well.
I can't help but have you on my mind.
You're fine like china.
This plate is filled with honestly and a side
of real talk.
Can you taste it?"
           You think you're clever?
  I hope you don't expect me to let down my
             guard.
Brandon: "I bet it's surrounded with barbs,
but I can find out how you're wired and
recalibrate it to turn you on."
          What makes you so sure?
Brandon: "I got it like that."
          A little cocky there huh?
Brandon: "No. I'm just confident."
I am mesmerized by his eyes and the way he
licks his lips.
I got to keep it together, but I can't stop the
gyration of my hips.
He has me excited.
I am astonished how he can have me like
this without a touch.
Brandon: "Let me show you what true love
is like.
Come with me."
   Are you just trying to get into my pants?
  Brandon: "No, but I wouldn't mind walking

I'll treat a guy right.
He'll be a king long as he treats me like a
queen.
Not to sound obscene, but majority of you
guys only want get the cookie.
I am not a jar for you to stick your hands in.
Bring something to the table that is
delectable and you'll get dessert in the end.
Brandon: "How long do you usually make
guys wait?
You don't seem like the type of girl to give it
up on the first day."
I see you got a good eye for quality.
Don't be distorted by my frame.
I'd rather let a guy picture what it would be
like to capture me in that light.
No one ever made it to that point with me.
If you stick around, you might get an
opportunity but don't take that as a
guarantee.
Brandon: "Since you been hurt so many
times, allow me to be the first to treat you
right.
I know it gets lonely for you late at night.
You're lying there with no arms to hold
you…"
Wait, no man needs to hold me when I got
God.
He holds me tight and it feels so right.
He gives me love that no man will match.
How can you possibly expect to compare?
Brandon: "You're right.
I don't compare, but instead of contrasting
why don't you start analyzing our
similarities?

Familiar Voices

Brandon: "Girl, I love you.
I'm not like the rest.
You can trust me.
I won't hurt you.
I won't ever let you go.
I'm not hiding anything.
You're the only girl in my life."

Man you scripted.
Do all men read from the same manuscript?
I heard these lines before and they all turned
out to be lies.
This guy needs to come with some new
material.
I hope he doesn't expect to be stitched into
me when I'm delicate as the fabric of time.
These lines drew me into shadows and time
won't erase all of monsters they created.
Brandon: "You are bitter.
You need to give me a chance.
How you expect to find the one when you
still stuck on your last?"

When all of you sound the same, how can
you expect to come first?
How do I know if I give you a chance, you
won't be worse than the last?
There's a reason I don't take chances.
I don't care to gamble with my heart. I'd
rather play with yours.
Brandon: "So you enjoy playing guys?
Are you on of those manipulative chicks?
Why do you think all men are just cocks?"

I play boys since they love games.

He looked suave and his smile…he hasn't
even touched me and already stimulating my
heart rate.
He said I looked very nice tonight and he's
looking forward to the evening.

emotions too soon.

He kept saying something smelt good; little
did he know that was my special perfume.

The sun went down and it was beginning to
get late.

The mosquitos were getting bad and I was
getting ate.

So, we got back in his car and he drove me
home.

He walked me to my door and to my
surprise, he didn't try to get me alone.

From then on, we went on more dates and I
learned more about him.

During that time, he even taught me
different things about myself.

He even was there when I got sick and
nursed me back to health.

I began to believe his words.

His actions appear to be true.

I just hope it isn't a disguise and he turns out
to be someone brand new.

Saturdays must be his day, because that's the
day he always tries to make plans.

He told me to wear my best dress that'll
show off my curves.

Hope he doesn't expect to ride these.

Although, he does look like the type whose
willing to please.

Let me get these images out my head before
this encounter leads to the sheets.

I bet he like them widely spread.

Enough of these thoughts, but they kept
reoccurring until eight.

That was when Brandon picked me up for
our date.

Saturday came just like any other.
Brandon came pick me up and we talked the
whole time to get to know one another.
He's smooth with his words, but I'm not
softened by silk.
If this is game, his chances of this date
continuing will eventually wilt.
He will be dead to me and on to the next.
The day was nice.
The sun was high.
I stepped out his car and swear I went blind.
We walked over to the biggest tree where he
had a blanket and a basket set up
underneath.
We had sandwiches he made over
conversation and everything.
We talked about life plans.
We discussed goal routes.
I interrogated him to find out what he was
all about.
We got on the topic of interest and what
would we do in certain situations.
That conversation transitioned into our pass
relations.
We covered everything from music to each
other's ambitions.
I even told him my views on men and he
reciprocated with his views on women.
I'm taken away by his current.
He's so deep and full of life.
He kept complimenting me on how it
appears I'm glowing when the sun hits me
just right.
I wanted to blush, but I refused to show my

The Manipulation

It's been a couple of weeks since Brandon
asked me for my number.
I assumed he was just going to stay in the
friend zone since he never made a move.
My nerves weren't worried.
Many men are intimidated by a strong
woman.
I'm not saying I possess manly
characteristics; I just know my worth.
For a man to discover my treasure he will
first need to understand my value.
My phone when off to the text from
Brandon.
He asked if we can get together tonight.
I was surprised.
I didn't think he would ever make a move.
Now I wonder if he knows what I like,
because I'm not your usual type of girl.
I enjoy the simple things.
I enjoy bowling.
We can go for a walk on the beach.
We can play in the sand.
We can go to an amusement park and ride as
many rollercoasters as our stomachs can
withstand.
I hope he doesn't try to be too fancy.
I don't like it when a man attempts to buy
me off.
A man's cash or how much he spends does
not impress me.
Spending some time will get me.
He suggested a picnic on Saturday.
Something simple, I like that.

His words tasted so good to my ears.
They were full of flavor.
He asked for my number.
Those digits climbed out my phone into his
contacts.
I caught a contact of his cologne and I
immediately felt high.
It smelled so good.
It made me feel so right.
I couldn't help imagining his lips....I would
love to take a bite.
I finally met a worthy challenger.
Hopefully he takes me high and he doesn't
blow up before my eyes.

smarter than I may appear.
Hold my attention.
The more time paid into getting to know me
will accumulate interest.
He has to carry himself; I refuse to raise a
baby.
My guy has to walk on his own.
Please possess correct grammar and word
usage because there's only so much slang I
will condone.
He has to show me some intelligence.
I'm turned on by a man's thought process
and attention to detail.
He has to be confident.
It will project in his walk.
It'll give me an idea of what will happen in
the future.
I refuse to be his backbone.
Please have a spine.
Don't be nervous to come talk to me.
My guy has to be well dressed.
It doesn't have to be the latest, but he has to
have a sense of style.
I don't think that is asking for much, but
according to some that is being picky.
A man should be able to fulfill my wants and
respect my standards.
I refuse to settle for less.
I am worth so much more.
Spoil me with consistency and I am
guaranteed to be his for sure.
Brandon approached me while we were in
the quad.
Four of my girls were ready to throw salt,
but he was rare.

Acquaintance

Come correct when approaching an
empress, because first impression is will
either make or break.
I don't give them time to fix their errors,
because men usually like to test me.
None of them ever passed.
They studied me wrong.
Most of them will never get right.
First of all, ask for my name.
He has to realize who he's talking to.
I'm not just an object he can use.
I have a big mouth and I love to run it.
My guy has to keep track of conversation.
My guy has to know what he wants, because
I don't have time for him to pick and
choose.
While he's trying to map out his wants, he
will be removed off my atlas.
I am not the girl to fall for the gangster type.
Slanging rocks will only get one stoned
dealing with me.
I get high off a man treating me right, but a
lot of men can't handle a woman that is
blunt.
My smart remark sets a blaze to their ego.
They find themselves smoked with laughter
from my girls.
He just embarrassed himself.
The guy has to know how to confront a girl
or there will be confrontation.
Don't try to con me in front of the boys; I
am
However, I just want to cruise as long as he

is in control.
He's like my favorite food.
I love fettuccini, but I he doesn't seem like
the time to be a chicken.
He doesn't seem like a shrimp.
I'm sure he takes charge.
His appearance is so electrifying.
I just want to dive into the waters of his
mind and become submerged within his
depths.
I bet he is deep.
I bet he has a story.
I want to open his book and pour my all
onto the face of his pages.
I'm talking to him from a distance, but I
can't pick up the pen.
I don't even know him and he makes me
feel right.
This boy has me feeling besides myself.
I'm standing next to me and we are both
gazing at a kingdom surrounded by
dynasties.
I feel my jaw drop and my girls are telling
me to pick it up, because he is coming
towards me.
I begin turning red like an alarm blaring.
I'm surprised through all these sirens, he
actually sees a heroin.
Although, I'm the one who's addicted and I
haven't even had a hit.
I need to stop acting like I'm going through
withdrawal, because I don't even know if he
will come correct.

collared polo.
This boy was bomb and I was ready to
detonate on the inside.
He was quiet.
He never made a sound.
I found him to be so profound, because he
would always have so many women in his
face but he never gave them the time.
He was clean cut from the finest rib.
He just appeared so tender.
He towered over me.
Lord, just give me a chance with him and I
wouldn't mind if things were to escalate.
He was precise with his language.
I want to be the only one fluent to speak his
tongue.
This boy was magnificent.
He was the extra special present that I just
wanted to rip the wrapping off of just to see
what unfolds.
He spoke and it sounded like thunder
clashing with Earth's surface.
His charisma was shocking.
I would do anything to be on his accord.
I find myself wanting to be wired into his
circuits.
He makes me feel like I am at a circus.
He is hilarious and I love to laugh.
His clothing announces he has a very
prestigious presentation.
I just want to be featured and casted in
anyway as long as I get the main role in his
show.
I hope he isn't the type to play a role,
because I am not down for the ride.

Brandon

I never was a big fan of art until I met
Brandon.
He was an artist made of his own work.
He was the Statue of David, because his
body was rock solid to match his toned
body.
His grey eyes were cumulous clouds.
He had a thunderous look that just appeared
so calm in the lighting, but they were
piercing.
He looked at me and I was stabbed.
This boy made my heart skip.
I find myself trying to hop scotch to his air,
but I'm actually afraid he'll see me as a
square.
I am mesmerized.
His chiseled jaw screamed confidence to
ears that were aware able to break free of his
enchanting voice.
It was soft and rugged.
I giggle at just the sound.
His smile were newly polished diamonds
that reflected my face.
I see me in his taste.
His complexion was sweet, tantalizing
caramel that I would not mind tasting.
I almost melted when he'd lick his lips.
This boy was scorching.
He was the sun on Earth.
I find it to be a shame that I see this guy as a
star, but I couldn't stop gazing.
His muscles exploded out of his

Brandon.

will one day have a son, whenever some of
the men stop being kids.
I don't want to have to end up raising two.
A man provides for his family and that is
something that any husband of mine will be
required to do.
Spend time with me and I'll be anyone's
greatest investment.
His revenue will be love and affection.
We will stock up on moments made when
conducting business and mixing it with
pleasure.
The equity of our assets will produce a
greater output when we limit all possible
liabilities.
Just be honest and we'll have a loving future
at the same damn time.
It's nice to dream.
Most of the men that approach me seem like
they're ready, but only try to sex me.
No, I am not trying to be down they're
nothing but a liar trying to get between the
sheets.
Age ain't nothing but a number but it's
about time someone turn these boys to men.
Then maybe we can do the unthinkable and
I'd be ready.
He has to be there to catch me just in case I
suffocate.
Happily ever after I can live with him for all
my life, and the fire we make will last until
the end of time we burn.
Just the two of us.
That was when I met this guy name

complexion.
Trust me, I won't hesitate to embarrass you;
especially in front the boys.
I'll walk off with a hair flip of my hair
without a care about his pride.
Actually take the time to ask me my name.
I am Nicole.
I am a natural girl that feels free when the
wind blows through my locks.
Doors will open to secret pathways in my
head when the right one comes and changes
locks, until then I am chained.
I am a smart individual.
I do not let any form of manipulation seep
into my brain, because mama raised me well.
I am a well containing a pool of wonders
that could be considered one of the seven.
I have a big heart filled with love for that
one sent from heaven.
I am nice and sweet, but don't try and
crucify my generosity because I will get
mean real quickly.
I am my smile.
I am pearly white.
I am my hips and thighs, but don't think
getting between them will help you discover
where my heart lies.
I am a queen that walks this Earth; given the
power to give birth so I am not meant to be
taken for granted.
However, I will please a deserving man
giving him whatever he wishes.
I will one day be a Mrs. and I

The Nice Girl

I never pictured myself as a Barbie, because
of the meaning behind the concept.
I don't want to be dolled up to be viewed as
a blueprint for sex by a man who won't
build me a home.
I don't want to be plastic so I can be either
disposed of or recycled by a man that
doesn't value me; I've got myself and the
man I'm in love with has love that's godly.
I don't want big breasts and a huge ass to be
perceived as my only assets; I have a
wonderful personality and I only give it up
in time when I see us making progress.
I don't want that ideal body type that is
keyed whenever a guy is bored.
My body is a temple.
It requires R.E.S.P.E.C.T.
That means, don't touch if unwelcomed.
I won't hesitate to pull the rug from under
his feet, and allow him to meet my words
that will stampede a herd of daggers into his
ego.
How's that for bursting one's bubble?
Yet, I'm really a nice girl.
A guy just has to come correct.
I won't give a guy play if he coming with
horrible dialect.
Don't call me "red", because I have a mocha

www.ingramcontent.com/pod-product-compliance
Lightning Source LLC
Chambersburg PA
CBHW062011040426
42447CB00010B/1996